What are Thinkologie Books?

At Thinkologie we believe in teaching language via stories. Thinkologie books focus on stories about notable people as well as folk tales that are classics in the country of origin. Stories bring cultural context and display regional differences as well. Each storybook has an interactive part to test comprehension. The storybook is in Kindle format as well as paperback. The accompanying paperback has activities to test comprehension.

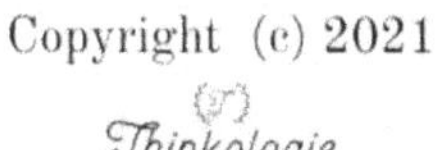

Brainstorming Activity

Guess what the story is about by looking at the title and pictures.

Write or draw out a brief answer.

The Story of Gulabo Sapera

Birth

Gulabo Sapera was born in 1973 on Dhanteras, the beginning of Diwali, the festival of lights. She was born in a Kalbelia family in Kotda village, Rajasthan. The Kalbelias are a group from Rajasthan who are skilled in catching snakes, charming them, and selling snake venom. When Gulabo was born, she was named Dhanvantari. Sadly, right after her birth, she was buried alive by the same woman who had helped her mother deliver her.

Gulabo's dad wasn't home when she was born. If he had been there, this wouldn't have happened. But when he came back, he and his wife decided to save their baby. They were brave and went against the village council's order to kill baby girls. Gulabo's mom and aunt secretly went out at night and dug her up from the ground, saving her life.

In Rajasthan, people think having baby girls is tough, especially for Gulabo's family, as she already had three sisters. Her family had to gather money for dowries for each sister, which was a big financial challenge. The villagers saw this as a problem, but not Gulabo's parents.

Because they saved their baby girl, the villagers didn't fully accept Gulabo's family as part of the village. Gulabo's father, following his instincts, used to hide the baby in a basket with snakes and take her to work. He was scared something bad might happen to her if he didn't do this.

Moving around the villages of Rajasthan was tough, but little Gulabo observed the world from inside a basket. Alongside, she kept an eye on the snakes. Strangely, she never felt scared of them. Instead, she would hop and have fun with them, even sharing their evening milk.

Gulabo's father understood that being away from her mother for long hours at six months old would make her hungry. To ensure she had something to eat, he fed her the extra milk that villagers brought for the snakes.

The Early Years

As Gulabo got older, she started imitating the movements of snakes. This led her to invent a dance that would bring her great fame. She had a flexible body, and her graceful movements caught people's attention from a young age. Her father changed her name to Gulabo because her cheeks would blush red while dancing!

Even though her family supported her, Gulabo faced difficulties. Whenever she danced, the villagers disapproved. They believed it wasn't right for women to dance either in private or in public. But Gulabo kept dancing despite their objections.

Recognition

At the age of 7, Gulabo attended a nearby fair in Pushkar. While dancing at the fair, some individuals from the Rajasthan Tourism Department noticed her and asked her to perform on stage.

Her fluid moves and grace captivated the crowds. On that crowded festival evening, she danced to enthusiastic applause.

However, even with this recognition, the villagers continued to object to her performances.

Royal Patronage

Soon, Gulabo began showcasing her talents on television. She proudly represented her home state of Rajasthan at different international events.

She made the Kalbelia dance her own by designing a distinctive outfit consisting of a black skirt and blouse paired with a veil. In Hindi, this outfit is known as a ghagra choli.

Once, the royal family of Maharani Gayatri Devi arranged an event and invited Gulabo to perform. Sadly, she couldn't attend because her village council forbade her from going. Maharani Gayatri Devi strongly supported Gulabo. This incident marked the beginning of a long-lasting friendship between them.

Gulabo moved away from her village's objections to Jaipur, a big city in Rajasthan. Jaipur is called the pink city because many buildings there are painted pink.

When she was 17, she got invited to dance at a Festival of India event in Washington DC by an important person. Sadly, her father passed away around the same time.

The villagers told her to follow a Hindu custom and not travel for 13 days due to her father's death. But Gulabo, like her father, didn't listen and went to the United States. There, she amazed audiences with her amazing dancing despite objections.

America was so impressed by her dancing that they kindly asked Gulabo to stay and teach dance there. However, she politely said no and returned home to India.

Surprisingly, her village warmly welcomed her back. The very people who had once opposed her were now asking her to teach their daughters. They admired her success and wanted their children to achieve the same.

Queen Elizabeth honored Gulabo with an award in 1985 for her talent. She got the National Unity Award from India's president too. Also, she earned the Padma Shri and became a UNESCO cultural ambassador.

Nowadays, Gulabo teaches dance to students worldwide. Her two daughters assist her in teaching. She's been on TV interviews and shows like Big Boss. She owns homes in various countries and is a role model for the girls in her village.

Gulabo Sapera champions women, not just in her Kalbelia tribe, but worldwide. Her drive is to empower women and eliminate biases in Indian villages. Her dream is to have a woman like her, named Gulabo, in every Indian home. She aims to establish a dance school in Pushkar, Rajasthan, offering formal education alongside dance training.

गुलाबो सापेरा की कहानी

गुलाबो सापेरा 1973 में धनतेरस, दीपावली के त्योहार की शुरुआत में जन्मी थी। वह राजस्थान के कोटड़ा गांव में कलबेलिया परिवार में पैदा हुई थी।

कलबेलिया राजस्थान के एक समूह हैं जो साँप पकड़ने, उन्हें मोहित करने और साँप का विष बेचने में माहिर हैं।

जब गुलाबो का जन्म हुआ, तो उसका नाम धन्वंतरी रखा गया था। दुःखद है कि उसके जन्म के बाद ही, उसी महिला ने जिनकी मदद से उसकी माँ ने उसे जन्म दिया था, ने उसे जमीन में दफना दिया था।

गुलाबो के पिताजी उसके जन्म के समय घर पर नहीं थे। अगर वो वहां होते, तो ऐसा नहीं होता।

लेकिन जब वे वापस आए, तो उन्होंने और उनकी पत्नी ने मिलकर अपनी बच्ची को बचाने का फैसला किया।

वे बहादुर थे और गांव की सलाहकारी सभा के आदेश के खिलाफ गांव में होने वाली नवजात बच्चियों की हत्या का विरोध किया।

गुलाबो की मां और बुआ रात के ढंग से गांव से बाहर निकलीं और उसे जमीन से खोदकर बाहर निकालकर, उसकी जिंदगी बचाई।

राजस्थान में लोग बच्ची पैदा करना कठिन मानते हैं, खासकर गुलाबो के परिवार के लिए,

क्योंकि उसके पास पहले से ही तीन बहनें थीं।

हर बहन के लिए उन्हें दहेज के लिए धन जुटाना पड़ता था, जो एक बड़ी आर्थिक चुनौती थी।

गांववाले इसे समस्या मानते थे, लेकिन गुलाबो के माता-पिता नहीं मानते थे।

क्योंकि उन्होंने अपनी बच्ची को बचाया था, इसलिए गांववाले गुलाबो के परिवार को पूरी तरह से स्वीकार नहीं करते थे।

गुलाबो के पिताजी ने अपने अनुभव के अनुसार बच्ची को साँपों के साथ एक झोले में छुपा दिया और अपने काम पर ले जाते थे।

उन्हें डर था कि यदि वो ऐसा नहीं करते तो उसके साथ कुछ बुरा हो सकता था।

राजस्थान के गांवों में घूमना मुश्किल था, लेकिन छोटी गुलाबो एक झोले में दुनिया को देखती रहती थी। साथ ही, वह साँपों पर भी नजर रखती थी।

अजीब बात थी कि उसे उनसे कभी भी डर नहीं लगता था.

जब उसकी उम्र 17 साल थी, तब एक महत्त्वपूर्ण व्यक्ति ने उसे वाशिंगटन डीसी में भारतीय महोत्सव के एक इवेंट में नृत्य करने के लिए आमंत्रित किया था।

दुःख से, उसी समय उसके पिताजी का निधन हो गया था।

गांववालों ने उसे संस्कारिक अनुष्ठानों का पालन करने को कहा और अपने पिता की मृत्यु के कारण 13 दिनों तक यात्रा न करें।

लेकिन गुलाबो, गाँव के बुजुर्गों की विरोधी कहीं, अमेरिका गयी। उसने अपनी कला और नृत्य की शैली से दर्शकों को चमका दिया।

अमेरिका ने उसके नृत्य को देखकर उसे वहां रहकर और नृत्य की शिक्षा देने के लिए धन्यवाद दिया। लेकिन उसने विनम्रता से ना कहा और भारत वापस आ गई।

अचानक उसका गाँव उसे स्वागत किया।

जो लोग पहले उसके खिलाफ थे, वो अब उससे अपनी बेटियों को पढ़ाने के लिए मांग कर रहे थे।

उन्होंने उसकी सफलता को सराहा और चाहा कि उनके बच्चे भी ऐसा ही करें।

1985 में क्वीन एलिजाबेथ ने उसकी प्रतिभा के लिए उसे पुरस्कार दिया। उसे भारत के राष्ट्रीय एकता पुरस्कार भी मिला।

साथ ही, उसे पद्म श्री मिली और यूनेस्को ने उसे सांस्कृतिक दूत घोषित किया।

आजकल, गुलाबो दुनियाभर में छात्रों को नृत्य सिखाती हैं। उसकी दो बेटियाँ उसकी शिक्षा में सहायता करती हैं। उसने टीवी इंटरव्यूज़ और बिग बॉस जैसे शो में भी हिस्सा लिया है। वह कई देशों में घर रखती हैं और उसके गांव की लड़कियों के लिए एक आदर्श हैं। गुलाबो सापेरा महिलाओं का प्रचारक है, न केवल अपनी कलबेलिया जाति में, बल्कि पूरी दुनिया में। उसका लक्ष्य महिलाओं को सशक्त बनाना है और भारतीय गाँवों में पूर्वग्रहों को खत्म करना। उसका सपना है कि भारत के हर घर में उसी तरह की महिला हो जो गुलाबो है। वह पुष्कर, राजस्थान में एक नृत्य विद्यालय स्थापित करने का इरादा रखती है, जो नृत्य प्रशिक्षण के साथ-साथ औपचारिक शिक्षा भी प्रदान करेगा।

Mark the Text

Use the following strategies to mark the text.

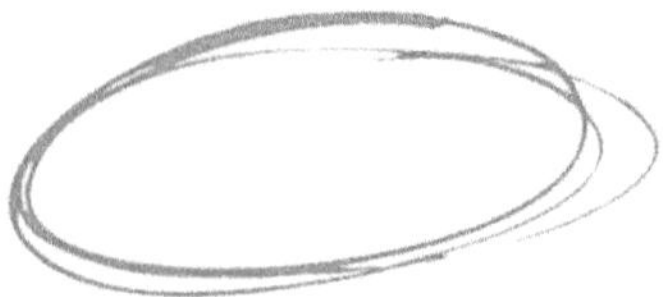

Circle content and look up the words in dictionary.com

Put a question mark near words that need explanation.

When did this story take place?

Where did this story take place?

What is the theme of this story?
e.g. love, slavery, war

Write the answers in Hindi in the following activities.
Use this space to write down any words you have found challenging to understand. Find the meanings of the words from an online Hindi dictionary.

Sorting Activity

Read the text. Find and place the words in the box

Adverbs	Verbs
Adjectives	**Prepositions**
Punctuation	**Superlatives**

Sorting Activity

Read the text. Find and place the words in the box

Nouns	Proper Nouns
Abstract Nouns	**Collective Nouns**
Definite article	**Indefinite article**

Questions

Fill in the blanks by circling the correct letter.

The Kalbelia are a___________ community.

a. tribal
b. snake charming
c. nomadic

Fill in the blanks by circling the correct letter.

Gulabo's ___________ buried her alive.

a. mom
b. aunt
c. mom's helper

Fill in the blanks by circling the correct letter.

The ________ rescued her.

a. mom and dad
b. mom and aunt
c. mom

Questions

Fill in the blanks by circling the correct letter.

The _____________taught Gulabo how to dance.

a. parents
b. snakes
c. teacher

Fill in the blanks by circling the correct letter.

When Gulabo was ___________ she danced on stage.

a. 8
b. 5
c. 13

Fill in the blanks by circling the correct letter.

The____________always objected to her dancing.

a. villager
b. school
c. parents

Questions

Fill in the blanks by circling the correct letter.

At the age of 17 she was invited to_____________.

a. Europe
b. America
c. Delhi

Fill in the blanks by circling the correct letter.

She returned to India and ___________.

a. Her village welcomed her
b. She started to teach dance
c. All of the above

Fill in the blanks by circling the correct letter.

She received the ___________.

a. Nobel Prize
b. Padma Shri
c. Oscar

Write a Summary

Create a One Pager

Draw and Label the Story

What do you think of the story? Write out your thoughts.

Culture Notes

Where is Rajasthan?

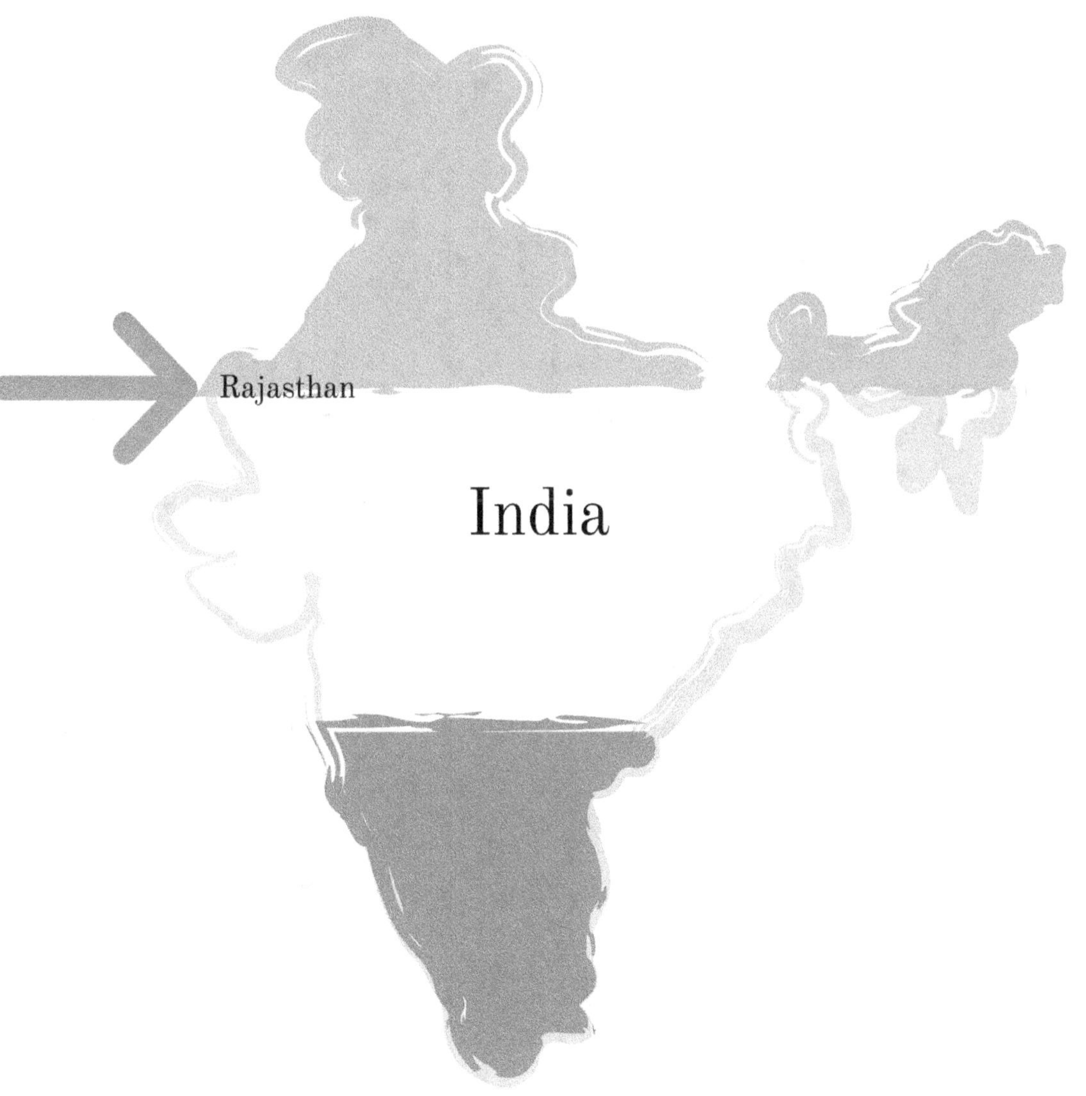

Jaipur

Jaipur is the capital of Rajasthan. It is called the pink city

because of the unique pink color of this fortified city.

Jaipur was founded by Jai Singh II.

Kalbeliya Tribe

The Kalbeliya tribe are a tribe of snake charmers that live in

Thar Desert, in Rajasthan. Their name comes from the word

'kal' meaning death.

Dance is also a big part of their culture. Today, both men and

women perform traditional dances at various fairs in

Rajasthan.

Gulabo's Outfit

Follow her @gulabosapera on Instagram

Thinkologie

Contact us

Our mission is to help other educators, coaches, and homeschoolers also!

Contact us for customized interactive books. If you want to publish your course into a book - contact us!

Our website:

www.thinkologie.co

Follow our author page

https://amazon.com/author/thinkologiebooks

We are also on:

Instagram @thinkologie

Twitter @thinkologie

Facebook @thinkologiemedia